D0909506

Gallery Books
Editor Peter Fallon

THE BLUE COCKTAIL

Audrey Molloy

THE BLUE COCKTAIL

Gallery Books

The Blue Cocktail
is first published
simultaneously in paperback
and in a clothbound edition
on 1 October 2023.

The Gallery Press
Loughcrew
Oldcastle
County Meath
Ireland

www.gallerypress.com

ISBN 978 1 91133 847 5 *paperback*
     978 1 91133 848 2 *clothbound*

A CIP catalogue record for this book
is available from the British Library.

The Blue Cocktail receives financial assistance
from the Arts Council of Ireland.

Contents

for my father, Tom

cocktail: a mixture of different things,
often an unexpected, dangerous or exciting one.
— *Cambridge Dictionary*

*We are tied to the ocean. And when we go back to the sea
— whether it is to sail or to watch — we are going back
from whence we came.*
— John F Kennedy

Emergency Cocktail

In the event of being stranded inland

Scoop half a pint of lake, river, or puddle water
    into a glass bottle — the recycling bin is full of them.

    Add a double shot of Hendrick's, a nip of Noilly Prat,
the shell dust from the pockets of your jeans.

The sea is saltier than blood by far, but prick your fingertip,
    add three blue drops as proof you're really invested.

    Grind some loose sandstone — that graveyard of miniscule
skeletons, ornate and intricate as Persian minarets.

Pour in a dash of brine from the jar of pickles in the fridge;
    an olive is nice, but a small sugar plum will suffice.

    To mix, simply spin on your heel, the bottle
at arm's length, until you're a blur of creased linen and limb.

After three days with no sight of the ocean, break glass,
    pour liberally over your face until it cracks
                           a smile of relief.

A Schoolgirl Dreams of Pools

I rode the early bus, hoisted high enough
    above the ditch to glimpse the yolk
        of sunrise glinting off the marl holes —
    imprints left behind by ice,
geese ponds littered through the fields
    from Screen to Curracloe
        like rosary beads in early light,
    the sea beyond like mercury.

All the way to town I counted pools,
    a breadcrumb trail played backwards,
        leading me away from home.
    By evening they were camouflaged by cowpats,
sheets of corrugated tin,
    discarded plastic sacks, or hidden
        by the shifting shades
of little whitewashed cottages.

And I could chart my getaway, pool by limpid pool,
    plotted out, pursued,
        checked off like early lovers.
    It figures, why I've always felt at peace
when wandering the rocky shelves
    of other shores, or searching out the green
        cucumber scent of quiet lagoons
known only to the conifers.

I dream of pools, finding them in places I well know
    possess no pool: briar-riddled streams,
        a tile of blue among familiar hills
    that might turn out to be
a kettle hole, or paternoster lake —
    pool dreaming — and, when I wake,
        there's still the faintest smell
of violets, or desire.

Marl, a drawn-out word; to say it
    is to hold, in your bare hands, the heavy clay
        as it holds you, unctuous and silty,
    in a closer understanding of what it means
to be a woman, not a stone.
    Is it true that the body pulls the water, or vice versa?
      Who would know? I began in a pool.
    I never got away.

Origin

Your first night in Ballyconneely
    and you've yet to take the shape of a glimmering girl.

    The cottage where you begin is thirty strides
to a shoreline fringed with coral sand.

This morning the fire, that will tonight become
    your fire, burned in the belly of a dab

    flattened in the weed, watching kelp
dangle from the ceiling of the sea.

Your father hooks the little dab. He cooks it,
    lightly floured, in a pan of butter, and kisses

    your mother. There are moths — of course there are —
and the summer moon is a bride's shy smile.

Tonight, in their pine bed, the lovers hear
    the sea gently rock against the shore;

    gow-ah, gow-ah, it says, *gabhagh, gabhagh*,
the spell of reincarnation, and you

are conceived, begun at last — two
    seeds and a flame in the shape of a fish.

The Gate

Two boys watch me peeing in the barley.
I didn't see them there, looking through
the gate.
One of them offers me a shiny 50p to view
my bottom again. I want that coin, but I say,
No thanks.
You see, my father could find that 50p
and he would want to know where I got it.

The Sheen

There is my soul there *I have seen it today.*
— Jason Allen-Paisant

At a fork in the road, the Rathnure side of Enniscorthy,
    my father pulls his Renault 4 in tight to the ditch.
        Two girls spill out, past nettles and brambles,
    to a stand of horse chestnuts.
The dignity of their leaves, veined and green
    as Savoy cabbage; spiked seed cases mottled
        where they fall; split, pithy seams
    for small fingers to worry.

There is my Autumn — prising a smooth seed
    from its bed, holding it up — *you beauty* —
        or the surprise of two, cleaved like sisters,
    each one flattened through sharing with the other.
And *this*: the seed glimpsed in its case, ajar,
    the pure sheen of it, shyer
        than glass, a diffuse reflection,
    as though dusted with flour.

Later we will dry them above the range, hard
    and dull for battle, pierce them with a nail,
        secure them with the rough brown twine
    found in a certain drawer in every kitchen.
We will swing them like morning stars
    and someone's will split, inedible nut meat
        like young wood, the range giving off
    its scents of mutton stew and oatmeal biscuits.

No horse chestnuts here, under a different sky.
    But early one April, driving from Queenstown
        to Lake Hayes, on a stretch of the Frankton
Ladies Mile Highway, I yelled *Stop*, and ran back

to a row of rhomboid forms along the road.
     I carried a fortune of nuts in the bowl
          of my sweater back to the hire car, their lustre
fading even before we reached the Sound.

An Old Man Then Is an Old Man Now

A girl in flares and a jumper embroidered with apples.
Your hand, too heavy on her head, unused to children,
used to wielding shears in Monksgrange gardens.

That day you wield a butter knife — worn
and mauve with age — at the strawberry thief
who peers around the back kitchen door

to ask about the mongrel cat. You spread
the butter thick on cuts of batch. *Too early for jam*,
you say, and spoon white sugar on instead.

Only one mug. She sips from an egg cup, saucer-
eyed from tales you pour into her head: the best boreen
to snare a rabbit, which branch of the sycamore

holds the blue-egged nest. When it gets late
you take her to the haggard to see the lemon moon
or to trace the lacy wormholes in the gate.

∞

She's heard that you're there still, time traveller.
Now she is spread too thin. The days blow past
like torn-off pages from a calendar

and you're the knife she jams in them to keep it all alive:
the girl, the loaf of bread, the pound of sugar,
the way some things are more defined in fading light.

What the Arborist Saw

A cat, among the finches, the sparrows and the wrens.
A cat, stuck, in the highest fork of a sycamore
the afternoon he scooped her in one fluid
movement into his jacket and kept searching,
calling down to the upturned faces of the boys,
No sign of the rascal, must have done a runner.

He feeds her fingertips of milk all winter
and cabochons of mackerel from his plate.
She dreams of fork-tailed swifts like origami
folded from the sky, their spittle nests
as hard and round as teacups.

They go to work each morning, arborist and cat.
He snips and saws; she walks the boughs
in zero gravity and, when he's rubbed the sawdust
from his eyes with the paddles of his thumbs,
he sees her carry every blue or speckled egg
in her ribbed mouth to his open palm,
and place each one, glass on velvet.

Skin and Blister

Dad would make me halve the éclair
and you got to choose —
perhaps it started there.

At school Miss Sinclair said,
She's not doing as well as her sister.
Mam said, *What's she got to do with it?*

Rathmines roommates,
failing to graduate in common ground
we mastered how-not-to cohabitate.

Since then we've gone round for round,
blows landing on rawness so often
our skin has hardened to a carapace.

But remember when, on our way to Sofala,
You've Lost That Lovin' Feelin'
came on the radio?

While the children slept in the back
we belted it out, filling the car
with rare harmony.

Mock Heroic

I lost my two best friends that summer's day.
  Before it lashed
we'd all trudged down behind the cemetery
to make a den beneath the weeping ash,
sucking fuchsia stamens for their sweet
nectar, plucking frochans on the way.
Raindrops, at first no more than a soft sound,
thickened up until their steady beat
had soaked our anoraks and pressed our hair
against our faces, on the holy ground.

Joe Ryan said, *Let's go back to our place,*
  watch a flick.
A funny look scudded past his face —
a summer cloud that went away as quick.
We shrugged, my sister and I, and agreed,
as it was much too early to go home
where Mammy would be cleaning still. And so
we trudged along the shiny gravel, beads
of rain collecting on our shoulders, loam
and cobwebs clinging to our sodden clothes.

Ryans' house had a hall with polished tiles
  of black and white
that you could skid along in socks for miles,
past doors to rooms I'd never been inside.
Orla said to Joe, *You wouldn't dare!*
But Joe was firm and, once the drapes were drawn,
he put the movie on. They both had seen
it many times before and didn't stare
as Claire and I stared at the carry-on
of Debbie doing quare things on the screen.

I warned her well but Claire told Mammy, soon
    as we got home,
and Dad went up to Ryans' that afternoon
to have it out with Mr Ryan. The comb
stuck in our matted hair when Mammy tried
to brush away what we could not unknow
and scrub the pictures from our minds. She sent
us, after dinner, off to bed and cried
at something on TV. And as for Joe
and Orla Ryan? They never spoke to us again.

Catching On

In the mid nineteen-eighties when I was twelve or thirteen, before the internet, when music came on magnetic tape, fed through a Walkman in a wax-jacket pocket, the way to learn lyrics was to play a song one line at a time and write down what you thought you'd heard, and after an hour of stop-and-start and back-and-forth with loops of tape unravelling, and wound back on with a pencil, there, on the page, would be your Joni Mitchel song or Leonard Cohen song and you could pick out chords on your hand-me-down guitar and imagine you were at a hippie festival with a daisy chain in your hair instead of shivering in the sitting room next to a just-lit fire with the centrefold of yesterday's *Irish Times* stuck to the fireguard to create a draught for the tiny flicker that might catch the peat briquettes and yield a sheet of flame into which you could tong coal from a faux-brass scuttle embossed with a hunting scene, and, as the centre of the newspaper turned light brown at first, then a rich sienna, before black smuts broke loose and fluttered like gothic confetti, and the lyrics were starting to catch in your mind, you'd have to drop the guitar, grab the burning paper, whip away the fireguard and bundle the smouldering wad into the flames, and if you thought Dylan sang *Princes, honest people, and all the pretty people drinkin' thinkin' that they got it made*, you could be forgiven, but when, years later, you discovered that the Stranglers' 'Golden Brown' did not in fact *lay me down with my manchiros*, even though everyone had sung along, and no one stopped to question what a *manchiro* was because it had the Latino vibe of a *bodega* or perhaps a breed of horse, that is when you would investigate this World Wide Web everyone was talking about.

January chill
yesterday's paper ablaze —
black snow rising

Ten Thousand Hours

Experts say it takes ten thousand
hours to truly know your subject,
which sounds like forever, but
is really only five hours a day,
five nights a week for eight
years. I mean, you could
finish your apprentice-
ship in shite-talking
in pubs by the age
of twenty-four, if
you were tall for
your age and wore
a little light make-up.

Ideas of Home

You make a strange pair, your father and you —
the middle-aged man and the teen, banished
for some mild transgression or other — arriving in rain
and a bluster that later churns up the Atlantic.

Your age gap confuses the chap in the camp site
and, tucked in McGann's, a man in a flat cap
keeps giving your father sly winks, but you let it slide.
Order pints. Scoff at their dirty minds.

The bars in Doolin are dim recollections of wombs
that have nestled your various versions:
quarter-light, warm scent of resin and hops,
and a feeling that's worth the long drive.

Fiddle and flute re-orientate and your tongue
feels as old as the drystone walls in the field.
We're having the mussels, he says, and his eyes crinkle up
when a mountain of blue shells appears.

Most of the tents are gone when you blow back after closing.
A few still billow and roll. Yours stands stubborn
but has taken the force in the shape of a rent
near your pillow, your sleeping bags sodden.

You never knew sleeping in cars was so cold.
Dawn comes at last, seeping through oyster light.
An obscure Verdi opera plays full-blast on the stereo.
And another four hours before you face off the full Irish.

You'll find you can never explain the idea of *home*,
meaning so much and so little. It doesn't translate
to shellfish and porter, casting long shadows into the small hours
wherever there's music and someone to talk to.

The Welsh have a word for this pull on the heart;
hiraeth, they say, *long sorrow*, where long is a longing
for where you belong, and sorrow a grief you gladly carry,
on your person, like a worry stone hewn from green marble.

The Entrance Fee

My father told me all you really needed
was the loose change for a Guinness Extra stout,
not a pint, he stressed — it's far too easy
for the man behind the bar to work out
your progress, swipe your nearly-empty glass;
no, the amber bottle hides a multitude —
or very little — permitting you to pass
a quiet afternoon perched on your stool,
long enough, with luck, that someone decent
might just happen by — a kindly stranger take
a shine to you — and shout another Guinness,
and, thus, he'd put in many pleasant days.
I found, with halter-neck and fitted jeans,
I didn't even need the entrance fee.

Smoke, Mirrors, Narcissist

We'd all ended up in a Leeson Street club called Leggs and we were smoking — me and a blonde in a majorette blazer. We were laughing hard at each other's jokes though we could barely hear ourselves think. *Is that Bono over there?* I shouted, and she looked, and I looked. I asked if I could light my cigarette from the tip of hers. We brought our hands close. She wore a cameo pinky ring just like my own. I leaned in and she leaned in, and I thought she was going to kiss me. My breath made a circle of fog on the mirror. I drew a little heart in it.

Rare Bird

Camden Street, Dublin

What you remember, in diamond clarity, after thirty years:
the low whistle of approval for your tuxedo jacket, the dance

of his eyebrows on finding, in your pocket, a flattened wad
of clean toilet paper — I mean, these places were filthy —

the smell of stale Guinness off the carpets, the reddish glow
to everything, the torn leather bench seats; the crowd,

five-deep at the bar; the way the fabric on the fronts
of the speakers pulsed to the beat; the fat,

smug feeling of having a cool guy on the hook,
the smell of Lynx, the first graze of lips, the blood rush,

the momentary clash of teeth — beautiful teeth —
the buzz of it, oh Lord, the want of it, hard as the whiskey

you'd earlier necked on a random car bonnet;
and the gaps in the record: how you got to the flat,

or whose idea it was to go in, whether or not
there was Nick Cave, more shots, or a spliff,

or in which room you lay down, grafted on the rug,
hands like pianists' beneath each other's waistbands,

your tongues pistons in the engine rooms of your mouths;
but you can still see his face when you shoved him off

and said *I can't do this*; how he said *neither can I*,
and that look, on the knife-edge of relief

and frustration, as he gave you the fiver for the taxi,
because *I don't think they take toilet paper*; how you saw him,

from time to time, always from afar, across a pub,
or outside a lecture theatre in a ring of pretty girls.

He was a twin, so you couldn't swear to his name
though you could certainly narrow it down.

A Photo of My Friend Reminds Me

We used to walk to an old phone-box in the Black Forest, not far from the hotel, to call home and ask for money. (A phone-box! My Mac keeps changing it to *phone-book*.) One night, while you were on the phone, I saw fireflies. They spooked me at first, floating like will-o'-the-wisps among the pines. One landed on my sleeve — a cold lozenge of citrine light — then flew away. You were telling them, back in Wexford, about the forty beds and our ugly pink uniforms. *Send money*, I mouthed through the glass, and you told them our German was improving, we were getting used to the food, but could they please . . .

You didn't speak about the sex, the new things we'd come to know. And we were cross when they told us that we wouldn't starve, poor dears, and next time we had a day off together we took the bus to town, busked on Königstrasse, you on violin, me on Spanish guitar, singing *Where do you go to, my lovely?* No one threw a coin, and you sulked a while and I smoked a Marlboro. So, we sat, instead, on the grass at Schlossplatz, braiding hair for a couple of marks apiece, enough for a *Stein* of beer.

We never touched the hotel minibar, apart from the two miniature whiskey bottles we stole, not to float a desperate message home, but to hold candles, and we sang all night, out of key, in our nicest underwear, up and down the halls, and the next day they moved us to another room.

Where *did* you go to, my lovely? I heard you'd gone and opened up a night club, first in Cork, then Poznan; always, with you, the music. The night I saw the fireflies — almost touched one with bare skin — I swear I heard a choir, a pure, clear score, that may have come from far away or, perhaps it was the sound of light itself, winging through the dark.

Night Diving, Koh Tao

Back first, into a bay of ink,
we sink beneath the longboat's
tapered silhouette, our soundtrack
the regulator's suck and hiss,
my air-raid pulse, and the off-white noise
of a million creatures on the night shift.

Daylight protests reverberate:
At night? Forget it, full moon or not!
But where the dream is worthy
love trumps fear and I find myself
drifting, dropping off in blackout.
A pair of stingrays ripples past.

A shoulder tap sparks dread:
my man makes the sign for *shark*,
pressing palms as though in prayer.
He holds them to his cheek
and tilts his head; *they sleep*.
(That much I know is false.)

A pack of tiny crabs plays draughts
on a table coral. The ocean wall
transforms beneath my cone of light —
a stadium of waving fronds, polyps
blooming: orange, tan, neon blue,
the first glimmer of a deeper desire.

City in a Blue Dress

Let me tell you what it's like to love a whore.

Awed from the first by her ankle-deep beauty at Bondi —
    named for the boom of her waves — I am knave

    to her self-tan armour. Dressed in her harbour,
cinched at the waist by her corsetry bridge,

she shimmies her way into indigo bays,
    cancans her skirts to reveal sequinned knickers

    that dazzle the whole fickle city with alternate
currents of *no* and *yes*. I love her best

in chiffon and lace when ripe jacarandas
    confetti her streets to lavender mire. She's a liar,

    promises Eden, and I see it flash by
every sunrise and dusk as I whisk

between suburbs by train, feel it draining
    away when she lures me downtown to diamond

    skyscrapers and lavishes favours on tight-
suited, glassy-smiled real-estate agents. I want her,

I *beg* her, to tell me I'm her only lover, but she never
    accepts my proposal. And we all throw her roses.

At Bottle and Glass Point

Where the water is brackish,
   not one thing nor another — the emigrant's curse —
      neither salt nor fresh, but varnish
   clear, these low-tide pools, embossed
with knotted snails and spider crabs,
   the opal gleam of bivalves,
      a flattened shell like the ear bone of a fish.

How I came to you: first love
   convinced a girl to leave her woods,
      her checkered fields, and cross a globe.
   Why I stayed: a white cove
on a creamy strand of pearls —
   Parsley Bay, Milk Beach,
      Redleaf Pool.

You are my ocean —
   blue cocktail of salt and sediment —
      but you are not my leaf.
   Feathered she-oaks — nothing
like the acorned trees I know,
   coastal rosemary doesn't grow
      along my memory banks,

and I dare not pluck your candy bells
   of fuchsia heath to suck
      the nectar from their stamens,
   as was once my childish habit
in the summer drizzle
   of another shoreline
      that, even now, exerts its pull.

Betrothal

I could start at the end, where I wave
    my legs in the air and say,

       You can fuck me now, if you want to,
    but that would be misleading.

In a previous scene I am driving
    in moonlight, the road

       a negative — a strip
    of ermine on velvet.

Some sounds are louder at night:
    the swish of gum leaves,

       each paper arc surrendering
    its minty scent.

For weeks I have practised,
    standing, hours at a time,

       on my head, the sun bending
    my shadow. The mistake —

as when making love — is being still.
    Trees rarely do this.

       On my first attempt
    they do not respond,

so I rehearse again, rooting
    my arms in sandy soil, my legs

       tilting towards the canopy, air
    flexing them at will.

The Red Gums are perplexed.
   Strano, they say — *strange*,

      and I can hear their caveat:
   To be a tree you must be born a tree.

I wasn't born a tree;
   I will have to marry in.

Transplantations

CAMELLIA JAPONICA

Like a shrub,
  you can kill a woman
      if you pull her,
wholesale,
  out of the ground.

Best chance —
  though no guarantee —
      is to cut her
back, go hard
  with secateurs and shears,

leave half of her
  to wither on the lawn,
      her carefully curated clothes,
her homemade cassettes,
  her glossy magazines.

Press your boot to a spade,
  dig out the root ball.
      Slice through her
taproot, strand it
  in red earth

like the cartilage of a throat,
  a pale larynx warning her,
      in her new world,
her place in the Garden,
  you will never belong.

BLACKBERRY

You have seen me here, writing love notes to the Wollemi.
Regardless, you must notify the authorities.
I am a weed of national significance.

Elsewhere, I am native — useful, even:
sweet belovèd bramble, *Rubus fruticosus, dris.*
Behold my barbed curtains, haven for the wren and finch;

see my floricanes — star-flowered, bee-nuzzled, oh so pretty
in the ditches — laden down with blue-black
fruit by autumn. Once, I was succour,

saviour, for the daughters of a famine-
stricken land. You fear my thorny daughters,
taking root in every blooming place my suckers find.

Report me at once.
Scrape-and-paint me.
Burn me. Try to rip me out.

ENGLISH BLUEBELL

No one else knows about the Monksgrange Woods,
only Helen. She brings me here to see the bluebells.

Wearing the same gingham dress in different shades,
apron-style with ruffles on the shoulder, we are wading,

knee-deep in indigo, we are taking off our sandals.
It's safe here. You could place your hand inside the hollow

of a fallen mossy limb and have no fear of venom.
Flowers can trick you into thinking you can take them home,

but these are not for vases nor for window pots. They like
it here, in shade and light, among the oak and lichen.

One day I will plant Spanish bluebells beneath a weeping
cherry. They'll be as near to the real thing as I can find.

The garden will face south, and my mother — sunworshipper —
will not believe that south can be a shady place.

Now the doppelgängers dangle in a different spring
in a front yard barely troubled by the sun.

That Spring, You Plant a Lemon Tree

And, after all this time, nothing fits
properly — not the sleek, tapered
clothes from *before*, the hard or pointed shoes,
the gauche embraces of old friends,
nor the daily rituals of an unlocked city —

only the gloves of sun-warmed soil,
your hands sliding into them to earth your body.
A lemon tree lights up the pleasure centres
like Grafton Street on Christmas Eve.
Kumquats too, and standard mandarins,

restoring zest with zest, bidding you
to run your fingernail along a bright, pocked peel,
inhale the oil, weigh the hanging fruit on your palm —
heart-sized, though not as heavy, encased
in pith, like a pot-bound root ball;

withdraw your newborn hands, red-brown from soil,
pink from whatever acid does to skin; leave
your small part in the rich humus, so that no one
can say you died, when you shine on
in the yellow fruit, a nascent star.

Whiteout

Three Sisters, Echo Point, Katoomba

No Sisters today, as I round the cliff path.
    The ghost of a gum tree floats at the limit of visibility,
        serene as a bonsai,

and all the debris
    in my eye's internal jelly rises   falls   rises
        on blankness —

an embryonic bird
    in the white of a fertilized egg in a porcelain bowl;
        and I seek the trident of rock.

Over the barricade, mist
    is dry ice at a concert, where the artists are ravens
        and a black cockatoo.

Do I trust the thick air
    to buoy my prone form over gum-bristled valleys
        to the stage

where Three Sisters wait in the green room
    of stratus? A tree fern takes shape like a martini
        glass in a smoke-riddled bar

and I half expect fiddlehead ferns to strike
    up Stéphane Grappelli. A pied currawong catcalls
        off-key as though

heard from an ambulance. Tiny wax flowers
    are the diamanté clutch I once dropped in an alley.
        My heartbeat is frantic,

a trapped sugar glider
    the stroke before laughter — which is to say slaughter,
       in the tongue of the kookaburra —

but I am not fleeing, just running,
    running blindly, in fog, with a heart as stony
       as Meehni, Wimlah and Gunnedoo.

Diaspora Blues

There's a mood on the way to melancholia
   right before the slide, the tinkle

      of light piano in a minor key, how the low-angle
   sun flatters your fickle skin,

how your face, reflected in a gallery window
   looks briefly refined,

      like Catherine Deneuve's — high cheekbones,
heavy eyelids shot in black and white.

You're glad you wore the fine black sweater
   and your heirloom velvet jacket

      though it doesn't suit the weather
and pearls are not in fashion

but neither is smoking, not even Gauloises,
   not real cigarettes — only e-cigs,

      blowing mood rings for ambience
on a shelf over the abyss.

One note from an oboe and this moment's
   the icing on the breeze block in your pocket

      and you know that in the likely event
of free fall there's half a Valium in a locket

around your neck that you haven't needed so far,
   and that's reassuring; by now

      you're so calm your chest barely rises, barely falls
and your aura turns aqua as you slip into blue.

String Theory

The universe can now be viewed as a vast symphony of strings.
— Michio Kaku

The man with beautiful hands doesn't understand
   he's a musician. He plays the theremin
      as he talks, oblivious

to the sound of a ghostly aria, one hand
   an arched arachnid, the other
      in delicate *vibrato*

resonating with the strings of some nearby,
   idling heart. Pushing back his hair,
      he strokes the air

and tells her, through the pixilated screen,
   why it is he cannot leave,
      tells her how, long ago,

in Okinawa and Honshu, they trapped the octopus
   in earthen jars called *takotsubo*.
      Oh, she would throw

her life away to enter such a jar and say its name.
   The chamber of the broken human heart
      assumes the *takotsubo* shape:

a heart within a heart, the muscle stunned by shock,
   blood spooling like the ink released
      in terracotta pots

when a creature knows its time is up —
   that *pizzicato* on the inner strings
      that could recall

the wingbeat of an ortolan above a vat of brandy,
    or a woman dusting places
        no one ever sees.

If she were to walk into the bay, past the dotted line
    of wrack, silt in her shoes,
        fabric sucking at her legs,

arms suspended by the elbows on strings
    no one else can see, what would the ocean
        have to say?

Ah, my love, my love,
    how I have missed you,
        how I have missed you.

And she would come again to amnion,
    lit with dull green light,
        a little courage required on her part

to flood the forests of her lungs,
    and on the part of the sea — to swallow hard,
        take her back.

Twilight, Rushcutters Bay

Kevlar. A tracking shot of silent sails.
Main, flat as paper; jib, a butter curl.
One flutters black and silver
loosened by a novice crew.
They slide past in their grooves
through a spawn of gaff-rigged dinghies.
It's always better than it looks,
a fisherman once told me
as I navigated busy waters.
Back then I loved to sail. Ask anyone.

Two swifts crisscross
the bronze-and-lemon bay
latticed with ripples
where the tide breaks on a weedy outflow
pulsing like some living thing.
Congress — that ridiculous act!
The nonsensical particulars of it!
Desire is the mother of beauty.

Past the cathedral of a Moreton Bay fig
where fruit bats cackle, organ notes drift
from St Marks on the hill —
O ye gifts of astonishment.
On a Spanish-mission facade,
Bougainvillea hangs out
her scarlet petticoat in the breeze.

Home, where arguments lie neatly coiled,
the way sailors leave sheets and halyards
ready for when the wind picks up.
A gust approaches.
The bay's surface darkens.

Eyes, too, do this.
Use the gusts, the old man said,
take the height when you can get it.
His hands smelled of bergamot and thyme.

Sea Clicks

From a cabin the *tac-tac*
    of halyards when the wind picks up
and roughs the bay: *sanctuary*.

Grey skies in Skerries, stirring
    a mug of tea on the salty lawn,
watching windsocks swing: *contingency*.

Six glasses clinking on a tray
    when the race is over,
sails flaked on the grass: *reward*.

A mouse beneath the berth,
    holding a Smartie in forepaws
that resemble tiny hands: *audacity*.

The epiglottis in my sweetheart's throat,
    moving as it only does
in deepest sleep: *contentment*.

My unloosed heart
    sliding back and forth
inside the bilge: *conformity*.

The gavel of the conscience,
    brought down in judgement
of the body it governs: *guilt*.

And the milliseconds
    counted backwards
to our unmooring: *acceptance*.

Learning to Swim

North Sydney Olympic Pool

NO SHOW PONIES

Fruit-shaped women of all ages parade
the changing room, breasts more pert
or sagging than mine, bottoms
more or less dimpled; swimming costumes
in safe hues chosen for colour-fastness,
not fashion; rubber swim caps
with tennis-ball seams
and latex bubbles I'd like to pop.
They banter and strip, nonchalant.
Under crêpe skin muscles are taut —
everyone is here to swim,
but this is not a poem about swimming.

FREESTYLE ONLY, SEE THE SIGN

Only the sky hears my splash.
Cornflower air fills art-deco arches.
Beyond — the harbour, dotted with goose-
wing boats I no longer sail.
My mind flips over with every tumble;
odd laps counsel *stay*, and Luna Park
is an over-embellished wedding cake.
Even laps urge *leave*; the North Pylon
of the Harbour Bridge pulls me, anchors
the whole tableau, the coat hanger
seen from beneath, private rivets
and secret workings revealed.

IN MY ELEMENT

Arms scissor the blue edge
of sky and pool and I'm unsure
of my element. Air snatched
from one, the other breathing
life into me, leaching fear.
Emerging lightheaded, amphibious,
I reacquaint myself with gravity.

Things a Streetlamp Knows About Love

The lovers mostly come in twos, recalling other animals,
    though I have witnessed three, and more, queued,

        slick with what the body does to brace itself for union.
    I have heard their sighs, relieved my glass has blown,

the dark a smokescreen for these happenings.
    I have seen the desperate ones who kneel —

        they are angels without wings. I've spied
    the street dogs lift their mangey heads, inhale

the night, then pad away to sate their own desires.
    I've strummed the strands of hair, flicked like whips

        when wives unravel, biting thumb or lip.
    I have dreamed of congress, to smash against another,

even for a snatch of time too short to catalogue.
    How I have longed to be a creature too.

To Die For

The cockroach that stays in the fruit bowl,
gorging itself, long after the sun has risen
and the house is awake, reminds me
of the blurry photos of that actor
from *The Wire* (what's his name?)
snapped in Rome with Lily James.
Or the fisherman, Santiago,
in *The Old Man and the Sea.*

For certain things, a creature
will give up everything, even life:
to land a massive fish, steal a mouthful
of ripe peach in broad daylight,
or run a hand through a pretty girl's hair.
One last feast on sweet flesh.

Audrey, at the Age of Forty, When She Thought She Was a Girl

After 'Dalí, at the age of six, when he thought he was a girl, lifting the skin of the water to see a dog sleeping in the shade of the sea.'

The day the world begins
   you peg the knave of spades
      to the spokes of my imagination,
  casting, in my wake,
a spatter-pattern
     of secret words:

verdigris, green of Greece,
   visible proof of our being here;
      stanchion (my sturdy upright fixture!)
  another word for stay;
anam, which is Irish
     for both soul and name.

I deal in lifting skin. Call me *trapper*,
  taxidermist, but I am neither.
   I am thief and you're my swag —
  your deckle-edge
and bow-tie eyes,
     your small profanities.

How long had you been lying
   like a message in a bottle
      in the ocean's midnight zone?
   And how did we arrive here,
wind chimes
     scoring the bright air?

An ordinary day.
  Too early for swimming.

No one prone on the pontoons. A boy,
brandishing a razor clam at his sister;
screams (or it might have been gulls);
        a mother weeping in the dunes;

and a girl, ankle-deep in soft wet sand
    flecked with wormcasts, eyebrows pinned skyward
        at how *light* it is — the heavy-looking sea —
    the way the clouds thinned,
then broke apart,
        this last moment of *before*.

What I Love

is afterwards, when we are reading — you,
   your magazines, and me, a slim book of poems,

     taking photographs of verses with my phone
   and sending them to one friend or another,

and I reach down — reading still —
   to slide my hand along my belly to where

     the soft hair begins, and deeper, until
   I touch the proof of what we two have made,

bring fingertips to face and breathe the mingled
   bleach-and-musky scent of loving,

     and all without you raising your eyes,
   or me losing my place on the page.

Long Haul

In the ink-black stratosphere, a sudden spider of lights, an earthly constellation, and I ask you, sitting next to me watching an old spy movie, what city this is, spread out beneath us, and you offer an unfamiliar name, population six million — bigger than the city I live in, my borrowed home. Below, in this place I've never heard of, people are eating prawns and rice, and throwing wooden balls at other balls, and making quiet or noisy love, and talking in whispers in houses overrun or abandoned, and reading instruction books or holy books or secret books of poems, oblivious to a plane far overhead. And I think of the time I showed you my favourite poem and you said, good God, I've never even heard of this poet; how you sat down, heavily, and kept reading, your mouth moving silently and your hands suspended in the air as though you were offering a blessing, or surrendering.

A Legacy to Seven Men I've Loved

To the first, a brass Zippo inlaid with the faint cartography
    of our nakedness;

the second, a maidenhair fern, the lacy fronds of which
    have graced the windowsills of every life I've lived;

to the third, a cloud confected from the contents
    of a beach ball, which is to say, nothing at all;

the fourth, two birds — Guilt and Regret: an ibis that pecks
    and an emu that ruptures your gut with its toe;

to the fifth, a bouquet of dock, nettles and dandelion clocks
    tied up with a Gordian knot;

the sixth, a biopsy of my shallow heart, taken by pine needle
    from the chamber with the trapped hummingbird;

and to you, Great Love, I leave a radio — a crystal set
    of galena and copper — fine-tuned to eternity.

The Rule of Twelfths

I learnt the ways of tides in a prior existence,
when I was betrothed to a fisherman.

It's why I don't go too far out on beaches
where a dog could drown if you lost track of time.
I saw a man at Sandymount, one summer,
windmilling from a distant sandbar backed

by Poolbeg's faded red and off-white stacks;
they still prop up the skylines of my dreams.
The tidal flow of water isn't *even*:
you reckon on proportionality — in punishment
or blame, and in saline pouring faster
into rockpools, swallowing the strand;

you take your bearings, estimate the rise,
not realizing half the shift occurs
in just two hours, catching you off-guard —
as life, or poetry, or love, can catch you
unprepared, expecting things to happen
linearly, not clumped, like dates or buses.

You are planning great important things
when all at once it seems those things
have happened in the past and you are caught out
on a shrinking bank of fond nostalgia,

arms flailing, desperate for attention,
poor Toto nowhere to be seen.

Postcards to Delphine

It's been a while. The children, the divorce. Has it aged you? Your clear skin! Sydney is bright and shallow as a low-tide pool at Plage des Cigales. Her harbour glitters like a necklace.

∞

Those summers, *ma chérie*! Memory, clear as vermouth — tan limbs on a blue-hulled dinghy, six hands playing Satie on the piano in your room, the floor lamp draped in chiffon. And the way you wore them; no one wears scarves here, Delphine.

∞

Red spatter of poppies in the fields — we didn't see them as omens. You were *thinking* about it, you said, and we laughed. I've heard you've lived many places since then, in draughty white houses, never far from the tinkle of halyards, lap of jetties or the herring gulls' cries.

∞

Admit it, Delphine; at fifteen a girl can love like a woman. That trip to Grenoble, you hovered near windows, green eyes fixed on the line where the mackerel sky disappears, and I knew. I forgave him. And you.

∞

I'd heard that you'd gone missing off Antibes. *A shark*, they said, although attacks are rare. I see you blood the waters where you stand, the smile that widens on your thigh, the flash of sunlight off the razor blade, the crystal liquid percolate through bone, as you become the sea.

Ta fidèle amie

Mackerel Panic

A bright, windy day between downpours.
At the end of the beach, a headland:
    the hunched bulk of it,
      the smooth meadow,
        the hard edge of trees
      tight as green velvet,
      the tilt of Bald Head in the distance collapsing
    like some elaborate sandcastle.
And cloud shadows racing towards me
  across woods, bare hillside,
    beach sand, then gone,
      running like their namesake
        in the Isle of Lewis, *rionnach maoim,*
      which all translations insist
    are cloud shadows, though the words mean
    neither shadow, nor cloud.

All this was sea bed, not so long ago
and these dark shapes bearing down,
    swimming straight through me,
      were blue shoals of mackerel —
        see them flicker and fly
      before unseen predators.
    It's only the wind, little ones, only wind —
  gone, like the plesiosaur, with its ten-foot skull,
banging the door on its way out of the Cretaceous,
  but you, little *rionnach*, still running,
    in go-faster stripes,
      from marlin and dolphin,
        puffin and whale,
      gannet and elephant seal.

It's harder to nail the translation of *maoim*:
I like to think of a wild consternation,
        a panicked eruption,
            an outburst of terror, a flurry,
                a navy-and-green pandemonium
            pierced by slivers of sun
        and a bluefin tuna chaperone
    watching for weakness
just as the wind watches for space
    where a cloud might be cleaved.

And if cumulus stared down the breeze
in its own version of a conversation of death
        rather than fleeing the scene
            would the shoal, too, turn
                its glittering face to the hunter,
            and jitter and stare
        through a thousand glass eyes,
    might it even lean in to the fear —
not full frontal, in defiance,
    but at a slight angle, as though
        leaning in for a kiss,
            that smallest of retaliations?
                You run ahead of your terror
                until you turn.

The Figure-Eight Pools

Burning Palms Beach, New South Wales

Like the light-green eyes of a man who uttered *stay*,
   these sinkholes, jade aquaria,

     carved by salt and wave to a sandstone shelf
   that formed around the time

things picked up again
   after one extinction or another. On the brink

     of a millennium, if another woman strode
   where I now stride, she might have had eternity in mind,

she must have stood on sediment,
   each grain a lithic fragment of an older rock,

     volcanic, from a wilder age, cemented into layers,
   or ground to fertile clays that host

the hanging vines and creaking fronds
   of giant cabbage palms that fringe the beach.

     Today two boys, bare to the waist, leap the pools
   which, by fluke, have formed a figure-eight —

a small infinity — the hollow sockets of a fossil skull
   staring at the shifting sky. A seal

     basks in the yellow light of a middle-aged star
   and the white webs of the sea rise,

looping over the lip of a continent,
   as they've done before, as they will again.

Girl in the Shell Midden

Balmoral Beach, Sydney

Even now we live among layers.
  Crumble or dig in the Burgess Shale,

    where Walcott sifted grains
    for clues to our demise,

or deep in cores of ice —
    aeons flaked in a frozen millefeuille,

    and here, under the overhang
    of a shell midden, where my daughter

crouches in a summer downpour.
    Plunge your hand in this cool floor

    and there are other girls, women
    gone to pumice, silt and sand.

    Where will *our* layers lie?

And what of all the shells to come?
    Sixty more millennia

    to whistle through, my daughter's
    cotton dress and sandals gone,

her bones and tongue forgotten,
    another stratum waiting to be found.

Once, I Was Claudia

Pompeii, 24 August 79 AD

They named me for my vault of secrets.
  I crushed coriander with a smooth estuary stone
    and breathed the green scent.

Ash was in the air. It made the drunkards cough.
  The blue amphora trembled on the shelf
    but I was not afraid.

At daybreak I cut my palm on a sea urchin —
  you could say, deliberately —
    to watch the blood fork down my arm

like the river at Ostia,
  to feel the fisherman press his mouth to a wound
    that gaped like a cockle at high tide.

It was a good day to bleed. I gathered
  them all morning — blue-black mussels,
    oysters with petrified frills and satin innards.

They simmered in the passum and harissa
  that my father hauled from Carthage.
    A man stood next to me eating snails, shell and all,

the yellow juice running down his chins.
  He smelled of the Lupanar. Heat rose from jars
    and through the earth. The city had a taste,

not sweat, not sulphur, but cardamom and honey,
  and the sunlight sieved through plane trees
    was thick and sweet. When it was almost noon

a cloud resembling a stone pine
    floated high beyond the hills. A rain of ash began
      in that ripe moment that hung
                  like a pomegranate.

Notes on Naming

My daughter tells me that the colour orange
is named for the fruit it resembles,
not the other way around.

The Droste effect, I tell her, is called after
not an artist or philosopher but a brand
of cocoa powder;

on the label, a woman in a wimple holds a box
of cocoa and the woman on its label
holds the same, *mise en abyme*,

and so it goes, this nested narrative. I tell her
that I follow on a line of eldest daughters
all named Hannah. If I squint my eyes

I see their forms unfolding, hand-in-hand, diminishing
like paper dolls to the horizon and beyond.
My mother — a Hannah too —

broke the line and chose a name she loved for me.
Grace eats her orange, slice by slice. She asks
what does Hannah mean? I tell her

Hannah means favour. It means grace.

Mirror in the Mirror

The child psychologist is   kind.
She says *fathers are close to their*   *daughters*
and your ex isn't ready for this   *diagnosis*
so we'll take it slow   *with him.*
How long's she been taking it   slow with me?
She says *it's about*   *acceptance.*
You have a rose and all   *you can do*
is help her become the best rose   *she can be,*
but you can't make her into   *a lily,*
no matter how much   *you want one.*
I say I never wanted   a lily.
She says, *it's like those two-way*   *mirrors*
in interview rooms; she   *can't see you,*
can't tell that her thorns   *have torn you.*
You must meet your daughter   *in her world.*
And, so, I probe   every brick
in the garden wall,   looking for
the sprung mechanism, the hidden   entrance.
I sit on her bed and listen to her   play,
her thin arms, fine hair, cut   in a fringe,
a reflection of me   at eleven,
but what passes   between us
is Handel and the theme from *Star*   *Wars.*
Weeks later I announce I've been   practising
Arvo Pärt's   duet
for cello   and piano.
But she packs her bow   away,
the score slides down   behind her bed.
The kind doctor talks cognitive   gaps.
I don't say I'm the one with   needs,
the need for my girl   to play
Spiegel im Spiegel   *with me.*

Years Later We Call It Happiness

'With numbers, are they adjectives or nouns?'
　　She often asks when I'm too rushed to think.

But in the car, a captive audience —
　　there's still another hour of freeway left,

slicing through bush, before we reach Pearl Beach.
　　She pulls my sleeve and starts to ask again;

I raise my arm — a stop signal. Mozart's
　　Ave verum corpus fills the car,

my blood, the cockatoo-embroidered sky;
　　it fills the gum trees to their brims. They spill

their music — green and brown and golden notes
　　that float like something you could almost scoop

with your curved arm, and I ask my daughter:
　　'Is Beauty a common or a proper noun?'

Stick Woman

In the park next to our block,
   on a floor of dry twigs and leaves —
      Grace and I, on low striped deckchairs,
a flask of water and some dates between us.
   The little ones run rings around the trees.

We are drawing Port Jackson figs, you see.
   My daughter says it's harder than you think
      to capture trees, to get them down.
Their bodies don't have endings, she says —
   they're wrapped around themselves.

That's the trouble with too few dimensions.
   I tell her you can trick the eye: draw the gaps and shadows,
      and the tree reveals itself. The artist too —
my fig has buttress roots like dragon's haunches,
   its branches curved and lush as daikon.

The little ones creep up behind us.
   We can feel their hot breath.
      They steal the dates, gulp the ice water.
My son makes stirrups of his small hands,
   helps his sister get a leg-up to the lowest bough.

She scrapes her knee, curls on my lap a while.
   Beads of blood appear on her dark under-skin.
      I dab them off, streaks of red sap on a tissue.
She takes my charcoal and loose paper,
   draws a stick woman and three stick children.

Later I'll pin her drawing to the fridge, next to Grace's,
   and my turgid tree. I'll rinse the lettuce,
      top-and-tail the radishes.
I'm no longer lush. I am a stick, a twig,
   kindling for their fire.

How to Love a Scribbly Gum

Study the zigzagged
     skin;
   decipher what you have failed
         to read;
  trace
    the code with your fingers;
      catch its strains on the cockatoo's scream;

probe knotholes
     with your tongue;
   smear the sap on your thighs and belly;
   curl
     naked in the hollow trunk;
  listen to
    the whisper of moth larvae;

reach
  for the heartwood;
      cradle it in your hands
   like truth.

Acknowledgements

Gratitude is due to the editors of the following publications where some of these poems, or versions of them, first appeared: *The Australian, Australian Poetry Anthology, Australian Poetry Journal, The Blue Nib, Cordite, Cyphers, The Haibun Journal, The High Window, The Irish Times, Island, Live Encounters, The London Magazine, Rabbit, Red Room Poetry, Southerly, Southword, Shot Glass Journal, The Waxed Lemon* and *Wild Court*.

A version of 'Girl in the Shell Midden' received the Hennessy Award for Emerging Poetry in 2019. 'Betrothal', 'Transplantations' and 'At Bottle and Glass Point' were commissioned by Red Room Poetry as part of the 2022 Red Room Fellowship.

'Diaspora Blues', 'How to Love a Scribbly Gum' and 'Postcards to Delphine', or versions of them, appeared in the author's chapbook *Satyress* (Southword Editions, 2020). 'The Gate' and 'String Theory' appeared in the collaborative chapbook *How Bright the Wings Drive Us* (Dreich, 2021).

I am grateful to The Arts Council of Ireland for a Literature Bursary that permitted me to work on this collection.

Thanks to the brilliant tutors of my MA in Creative Writing at the Manchester School of Writing, Manchester Metropolitan University, Malika Booker, Kim Moore, Andrew McMillan, Helen Mort and Michael Symmons Roberts, and to my fellow MA students — I'd love to start all over again.

To the book's first readers, Bobbie Sparrow, Morag Anderson, Alison Gorman, Daragh Byrne, Barbara DeCoursey Roy, Maeve McKenna and Ricky Ray, for invaluable feedback on drafts of these poems and the collection as a whole, thank you.

My gratitude to the late Kevin Higgins — one of the kindest men who ever wrote a poem — whose online workshops prompted several poems in this collection.

I'm indebted, always, to the generosity and support of Peter Fallon and the team at The Gallery Press.

My love to my children, Grace, Harry and Milly, and to Graeme, for loaning me out to the muse.

Notes

'A Photo of My Friend Reminds Me' is for Andrea.
'Long Haul' is for Maeve.

page 15 This poem alludes to Michael Longley's 'The Leveret' and W B Yeats's 'The Song of Wandering Aengus'. *Gabhagh* is the Irish word for conceived.

page 22 A frochan (*fraochán* in Irish) is a wild bilberry found in Ireland in summer months.

page 24 Bob Dylan, 'Like a Rolling Stone': 'Princess on the steeple and all the pretty people, they're all drinkin' thinkin' that they got it made.' The Stranglers, 'Golden Brown': 'lays me down, with my mind she runs.'

page 39 *Dris* is the Irish word for bramble, briar or black-berry.

page 43 In Aboriginal dream-time Meehni, Wimlah and Gunnedoo were the three beautiful sisters of the Katoomba tribe turned to stone by a witchdoctor to protect them from harm.

page 47 '*Desire* is the mother of beauty' riffs off 'death is the mother of beauty' from Wallace Stevens' poem 'Sunday Morning'.

page 62 *Rionnach maoim* features in Robert Macfarlane's *Landmarks* (Penguin, 2015).

page 63 'conversation of death' is a term coined by Barry Lopez to describe what occurs when wolves and prey remain absolutely still while staring at each other (*Of Wolves and Men*, Scribner, 1978).

page 66 This poem was prompted by the story, 'Pompeii "fast food" bar unearthed in ancient city after 2,000 years' (Angela Giuffrida, *The Guardian*, March 2019).

page 72 The Scribbly Gum is a eucalyptus tree, endemic to Australia. Its bark is marked with zigzag 'scribbles' created by the tunnels of the larvae of the Scribbly Gum moth.